SEASONAL MOODS

Edited by

Heather Killingray

First published in Great Britain in 2000 by
POETRY NOW
Remus House,
Coltsfoot Drive,
Woodston,
Peterborough, PE2 9JX
Telephone (01733) 898101
Fax (01733) 313524

HB ISBN 0 75430 843 X
SB ISBN 0 75430 844 8

FOREWORD

Although we are a nation of poets we are accused of not reading poetry, or buying poetry books. After many years of listening to the incessant gripes of poetry publishers, I can only assume that the books they publish, in general, are books that most people do not want to read.

Poetry should not be obscure, introverted, and as cryptic as a crossword puzzle: it is the poet's duty to reach out and embrace the world.

The world owes the poet nothing and we should not be expected to dig and delve into a rambling discourse searching for some inner meaning.

The reason we write poetry (and almost all of us do) is because we want to communicate: an ideal; an idea; or a specific feeling.

Poetry is as essential in communication, as a letter; a radio; a telephone, and the main criteria for selecting the poems in this anthology is very simple: they communicate.

CONTENTS

SHE BREATHES

She stands barren.
Before the first sprinkling
Of snow falls
On her lush green valleys,
She breathes,
Reaching up and grabbing
The last rays
Of the cold morning sun
Before it fades;
Cascading her
Into winter's
Dark
Frozen
Abyss.

She stands barren.
Before winter's frozen breath
Blows north
Across her lush green valleys,
She breathes,
Sitting golden, soaking up
The last rays
Of the cold morning sun
Before she fades;
And her last days
Of summer
Crumbles
Into
Dust.

Marcus Tyler

SAD (SEASONALLY ADJUSTED DISORDER)

I have worn this shroud
For long enough;
The darkness of death
Has clipped my wings,
Weighing down pasty white flesh
Cold, prodding like fingers
Kneading, massaging skin
Into shivering numbness.

I would hibernate
Sleep until the warmth of spring
Brings life and colour again;
But I am not allowed escape
I must suffer a polar landscape
Inside nature's fridge;
Live through this cleansing freeze
Dull and lifeless like the trees.

Nigel Bangert

SPRING THAW

It's milder today.
A wild wind
soughs in the beeches,
where crows congregate
to debate their next move.
At ground level,
pheasants in brocade outfits
saunter like gents
out for a constitutional,
and the thickets echo
with their plangent conversation.
All that demoralising snow
and immobilising frost
are gone from the raw soil,
and the gardens
stretch their arms out wide
and breathe in warmth.
All that remains of winter
is a sprinkling of snowdrops
and the lustre of aconites,
happed in shining green.

Ken Angus

SUMMER COMES

Summer arrives swift
with hayfever
and desire to be fulfilled.
It builds
as the dawns get shorter
light lasts longer.
Heat gets stronger and stronger
and we wait for the cloudless sky,
the still breeze.
Heat wains
and so soon afraid
on a cold winter's day
or night,
there is no telling the difference.

Summer comes fast.
Another hot day needing you.
Another winter searching for you.
Another setting set
and the hero declines to enter stage.
The sun is here now
and takes its short time to burn out.
The winter plays out its dark act.
And the cold creeps in
as quickly as the hottest day is had
some when in July or August.
Then it is gone
as quickly as the sun enticed you to live.
As tragically as a summer without love.

Edward Harlow

LEAVES

The flame is red
Consuming all, destroying all
Ashes remain, grey as death
Blown in the wind, scattered wide.

The torn branch is green
Leaving the scar that never heals
The limb is gone but feels the pain.
A limbo full of nothing.

The winter sun is pale yellow
No warmth, no heat, but brightly sad.
Remembering when it had life
A million miles ago.

And now there is a winter wind
All the leaves are gone
The red, the yellow and the green
They lie there tender on the grass
And lovers walk on them.

The trees are skeletons
Still beautiful but dead.

Frank Harling

SEVEN SEASONS

Frost came in the night it stole my world
Over mountain tops a strange mist curled
Images of spring once so prestinely true
Across the landscape there's a cold frosty blue
Tell me not mournful seasons of thy numbers
Our souls are dead where pollution slumbers
For our life's are but a cold empty dream
And things are never what they seem
The wind of change she has no soul
And our destruction's become her goal
There is a reaper his name is death
He stalks this world with destructive breath
Trees and flowers where they grew between
In the year 2000 are no longer seen
There is no light in earth or heaven
And angels of the night bring season seven
Where the tall oak trees branches stand
Comes cruel the sea to cover the land
Nature's damp cold touch forbidding to aspire
Brings down dark misty fogs and forest fire
The winds and snows bring melted flood
Storms and rains bring trains of mud
She arcs her back she screams her pain
Bringing season seven to wax and wane
Ice age come'th Mother Nature dims her lights
Cold barren world without any nights
She sends her wrath and immortal fears
World covered in darkness in apocalyptic years.

Ann Hathaway

LET ALL THE INHABITANTS OF THE WORLD STAND IN AWE OF HIM

We come O Lord before you
in humble adoration

As we think of lofty mountains
and the beauty of creation

No human hands could make
the wonders that we see

The colours of the flowers
and the tall majestic trees

And we stand in awesome wonder
at the work of your hands

And thank you Lord our God
that you designed us in your plans

So we lift our hands and voices
to the master of creation

We come O Lord before you
in humble adoration

Ann Langley

AUTUMN BREATHES AGAIN

Now Autumn breathes again
A merry cooling chill,
Laughing through the treetops
Blowing leaves at will.
Crispy leaves a swirling,
Swirling in a trance,
Down village lanes and garden paths
Within an Autumn dance.

Robin Redbreast singing
From the cold wet mound,
Friendly cherished caller,
Autumn's welcome sound.
Saints are now remembered
In the church nearby.
While rainbows bring great joy and love
Within the Autumn sky.

Now Autumn breathes again
Our Summer leaves the stage,
True splendour bows her head,
Beauty turns the page.
Change of heart and colour,
Time for wax and wane,
Let nearness seek its love and warmth
Within the Autumn rain.

Peter James O'Rourke

SEASONS

All seasons arrive with their different kinds of magic.
Some quite joyful - others quite tragic.
You wish to pocket it all as year covers year,
But are told not to be silly as it's bound to come again, never fear.

Winter days are here and all one thinks of is
How those glorious days of summer had ever come to this.
But if one looks closely I'm sure they will find,
Plenty around to occupy the mind.

Spring comes next and all bursts into bloom,
Things look overcrowded - but somehow you find room.
It's lovely to see delicate things grow big and strong,
For you know they will help those dusty days of the next season along.

Summer days come and seem to be enjoyed the most,
Perhaps a few hours can be spent by the coast.
Lazing around on a beach doing nothing all day,
Or drinking in knowledge in many a different way.

Autumn appears, the season I like best,
For one sees flora and fauna don their prettiest dress.
The colours that appear at this time of year
Intermingle so well, I'm always sorry to see them disappear.

Betty Green

HAMPSHIRE LANE

The soft-lit ending of a summer's day.
Long tree shadows stretch across the road
In lines that count all those who pass this way
Through these weightless stripes of fate's bar-code
Until, behind a line of cars ahead
I stop, and as the noise of movement falls,
I hear from woodlands tinged by sunset's red
The noise of bar winged pigeons' settling calls.
The plant scents change as dusk brings on the dew
Then round the bend, the scene of the delay,
And past the grim faced men who wave us through
While others cut the crumpled steel away.
And back-lit, stark against the sunset sky,
Above their heads, a drip bag held up high.

T Robertson

THE GARDEN IN AUTUMN (THE FALL)

The autumn not an end
of the gardening year,
A beginning of things to come.
The beauty of a billion leaves
a tidy up for the coming year.

How to plan what to put in
the many bulbs, the many plants.
Get in fresh air, wear your old pants.
Whoo - the kids have just been
in black cept' their eyes
want some cash, for Hallowe'en
(ready made guys for the Nov 5th bash).

Back to the drawing board,
get one's feet up,
too late now to do out today
close one's eyes, think and surmise.
Relax and enjoy,
the garden as well
is there to enjoy.
We don't want a prize
don't expect the best.
We'll just do our bit
and thank God for the rest.

A beautiful garden though
does need some work.
Now it is important
we have relaxing work.
Put things in perspective.
We'll do that tomorrow
and try not to shirk.
We are not lazy,
so try not to smirk.

Dan Brown

RAIN

Loud sang the bird in the
Juniper tree,
Singing so merrily,
Bursting with glee.

Singing of morning, and
Haloed with gold,
Sweet was the song he so
Merrily trolled.

Brilliant the morn, and the
Bird singing gay -
Swiftly it darkens to
Wintry grey.

Clouds o'er the sun, and the
Rain falling free -
Silent the bird on the
Juniper tree.

List for his song and you
Listen in vain -
All you will hear is the
Beat of the rain.

Henry Harding Rogers

AUTUMN GLORY

A look out of my window and I espy
Autumn in her glory has arrived,
Leaves on paths and along the drive
This season cannot be denied.

Most folk now become depressed
Thoughts of rain, and so much coldness,
Even though the nights draw in -
I still enjoy the autumn stillness.

To battle home in wind and rain -
To see a fire and kettle boiling,
Evenings spent by fire relaxing
Collecting thoughts from daily earnings.

Sometimes on a bright chill morn
We walk through leaves and watch the dawn.
Memories of childhood all around
Sounds of running, playing still abound.

Autumn again brings fruit abundant
Blackberry and apple to pick whilst walking.
Shall I make a pie or crumble?
Why not both, make tummy's rumble.

God makes each season rather special
Some prefer, spring, summer, and even winter.
To me the colour and hue of autumn
Makes this season just phenomenal!

Freda Symonds

SOUTH WEST SEASONS

Winter's not a favourite time
So dark and dull and grey.
If through the clouds the sun would shine
We'd have some better days
The days so short - the night's so long
Come along spring - let's have some song.

The winter is over - it's passed and gone
Birds are singing at last
The air is filled with their various song
And the bulbs are coming up fast
The days are longer with sunshine and showers
Spring is here and so are the flowers.

Not to be outdone - the summer has come
Can she with spring compete?
She will continue what spring has begun
And give us a little more heat
Long sunny days and evenings cool
Just the climate to visit the pool.

And autumn tries to be benign
Many good days she can offer
The weather she gives so often quite kind
We gladly accept what she offers
Enchanted are we with her colourful shows
As she paints the landscapes in yellows and golds.

Dennis Skirton

ROUND IN CIRCLES

Icicles melt with winter's retreat,
Earth is stirring in sign of new life,
Growing stronger, impatient to greet
A new dawn, casting off the strife
Of dark cold days, bursting to bring
The wonder of spring.

Visions of colourful blooms display
Their vibrant hues and heady scent,
Sunshine draws the radiant array
To lift their heads in vain content,
To stir the senses and warm the heart,
As summer plays her part.

Russet, copper and gold adorn
The players in the pageant of change,
The time has come when harvest dawn
Will cover all to rearrange
The countryside with regal grace,
As autumn glides in place.

A final leaf falls to shivering earth,
Beneath darkened sky and cold winds shout,
And naked landscape awaits rebirth
In slumber, whilst heaven breathes out
Crystal breath on land and trees
For winter's shimmering freeze.

Pamela Dawes

LOOE IN WINTER

Winter time's a quiet time
In this small town of Looe
Visitors have often asked me
What is there to do?
When all the summer crowds have gone
No boats are on the river
The days go grey and rainy
And cold winds make you shiver.

Then it's time to gather 'round the fire
With friends who sit and talk
Or curl up with a favourite book
No need to watch the clock
For there's no rush to go to bed
And no rush to get up
Now my boys are grown and gone
I've only got my pup
And so I'm free to spend my days
In pastimes I enjoy
Reading, writing, playing games
Or driving down to Fowey
To Lostwithiel for auctions
Talland Bay Hotel for tea
I love Looe in the winter
It's never dull for me.

Betsy Van Wormer

END OF A SUMMER

Cricket stumps lie sealed in a canvas bag
The wind softly sighs for it to is sad
The snapdragon's jaws are old and cracked
No more picnics to be unpacked.

A thunderstorm shakes the trembling sky
Which was infinite blue for most of July
But now the leaves on branches are stripped
Spiralling downwards to an earthy crypt.

The corner cafe huddled in the shade
Renowned for its cheap lemonade
Has shutters up and blinds are drawn
Anticipating autumn's ochre dawn.

The morning haze and river mist
Crossed by butterflies which no longer exist,
The river like quicksilver snaking unseen
Through countless meadows which were golden and green.

Memories of a season which was warm and dry
Sadly we accept another summer gone by
As we twist our eyes towards an overcast sky
And shudder at winter's oncoming cry.

Mark Evans

CYCLE OF LIFE

In the forest all is dark,
all hushed and waiting, for the dawn.
Sounds the herald, song of the lark
announcing a new day is born.
Benign and gentle blows the breeze
to stir the new born foliage.
A shaft of sunlight through the trees
and spring has turned another page.

Long summer days, and all serene.
The air is warm; the grass is green.
A glimpse of autumn's fruit is seen
to show us where the bees have been.

And on to autumn's bounteous store.
Who could wish for anything more?
Flagging now are the trees that bore;
Tattered are the dresses they wore.

But nature needs a time to rest
when dreary nights are dark and cold:
While roots perform their endless quest
ensuring leaves once more unfold.

Grace Mills

WINTER COMES

Winds from the north
Then blows the snow;
Thus winter comes,
Small creatures know!

The holly berries, glossy red,
Add colour, to a dowdy bed;
Where once, more colour was enjoyed,
Before insidious frosts - destroyed!

The migrant swarms have gone - and leave,
Nought but a memory, to bereave!
The white decked firs and pines remain;
To mourn the roses, which were slain!

The birds are few, with will to sing,
While nature waits - the birth of spring!

Ron Bissett

CRYSTALS OF THE DEEP

White peaks surround a winter lake,
Protecting a shaped cut glass surface,
As the dawn rises, a casket of discovery unlocks itself,
Shining iced diamonds and sapphires,
A blue jewel of our heritage,
Sunset is heaven gazing on this treasure.
Darkness becomes the background for fantasies to come alive,
Streaks of lazerlight, dancing and sparkling,
The luminous moon is smiling,
Thoughts of contentment shared.
Time itself, changing formation,
Seasons folding into place, species of the wild accommodate,
Hibernation brings isolation, for self preservation.
A magical vision, as curtains of green are pulled away,
Frosty icicles from dewdrops hanging,
Blankets of snow, concealed chestnuts lay,
Secrets of a squirrel hidden,
Colours blend to climates of different nature.
Imagination expands so rapidly,
No limits for developing emotions,
Logs seem to burn so intense within my heart,
The coldness of despair and grief can not enter.
Crystals of the deep.
Riches beyond my dreams,
Landscapes and clear skies, wonders of a lakeside view,
Point to a location, only found printed on a map,
Inside my very own . . .
Peace of mind.

Nigel Astell

MEMORIES

As I have said before
We did not really notice
The seasons during the war
We were just glad to be alive
To be with our friends and family and survive.

Anyway all the seasons have good points.

The dark cold nights when we were small
Mum let the fires in the grate flicker very low.

Brother Tom had his door open, so did I
The firelight flickered like magic
And we played *I spy.*

The spring and summer when there was time
Regents Park Hampstead Heath Parliament Hill
Primrose Hill and Ken Wood
Mum always busy, dad working
She always seemed to find the time.

Then the fall

Well, what can I say, Indian Summer during the day

But you could walk for miles, days shorter OK,
The days can be unbelievable I'd say.

My aunt Nell and me
I loved to walk among the leaves I was so happy

During the war Bill was in hospital in Somerset
In September, before going back to Germany
It did help that the weather smiled on us
Nobody ever seemed to make a fuss

You just looked out of the window if you needed
A brolly anyway.

Phyllis O'Connell (Hampson)

THE WEATHER VANE

It swivels with breezes
Like soft blown kisses;
alternates with currents
like men that take to seas.

Today brings on tomorrow
as newscasters predict
the millennium bug,
asteroids and other sorrow.

The weather vane keeper died,
only the rusting metal remains,
and there is no more
catching wind at first light.

The fisherman came to me
requesting its re-installation
for its forecast is unparalleled,
indispensable its accuracy.

Now, when winter comes,
fishermen look the other way,
winds no longer whistle
through its long rheumatic day.

Raymond Fenech

MOTHER NATURE

Mother Nature battles on
Her strength and power is so strong
She wakes each day
But never sleeps
We think the world is ours to keep
She is the leader
She is the one
She's in control of the moon and sun
A hurricane here, an earthquake there
She does not want those buildings there
We're ruining the planet
It's not ours to own
All these changes she won't condone
The earth's lungs; these are the trees
Without these we could not breathe
It's conscience us humans lack
Beware, Mother Nature is fighting back.

Lisa Bennett

HARVEST SONG

Some sun, some rain, some warmth, some chill.
Grass becomes adorned with morning jewel
Shining to Sol's smile in dwindling days
While nature with her paintbrush plays.
Masterpieces extended during night,
Leaves' gilded hues match dramatic red
Majestic purple joins humble brown
Foretelling what must come quite soon.
Berries glow to feed the feathered flock
Wind's murmur stirs the crop to drop.
Plump nuts for squirrels in the wood
Who busily store their winter food.
Baled hayfields bristle stubble now
Till ploughs arrive feeding gull and crow.
Muddy stream, chuckle, bustling on,
Flirting and frolicking with each stone.

The countryside yawns and takes repose
As voices rise in harvest praise.

Roma Scrivener

CHANGING SCENE

White, shining bright
Transforms the sight of trees and fields and hedgerows
Quiet and still
The wind is chill
Although a watery winter sun glows.

Green, changing scene
The wind is keen, but now a warm spring sun shines
Cuckoo's here
Wild flowers appear
Primroses, violets, celandines.

Blue, yellow too
And every hue of blossom, shrub and flower in bloom
Blue sea and sky
Ride, sail or fly
Away from that small bed-sit room.

Gold, now behold
The year grows old, mellows and ripens as the hues mature
Warm balmy breeze
Fruit-laden trees
And golden corn fields ripe for harvest store.

White, shining bright
Wrapped warm and tight against the biting wind that blows
Sit by the fire
Hear the church choir
Sing Christmas carols, whilst the yule log glows.

Estelle James

HOSTILE NATURE

Nature's elements, as times so savage,
Forest earth and sea they ravage,
Roaring and snarling with awesome might,
Terrorising all through day and night,
Electric storms rend the night apart,
Volcano's disgorging their fiery heart,
Twisting tornadoes consume all in their path,
Spewing it out in their terrible wrath,
Hurricanes flattening all they behest,
Avalanches sweep all aside down a hillside,
Earthquakes felling cities far and wide,
All causing carnage, like a beast on the prowl,
With thunderous roar or ominous growl,
Man with nature just can't compete,
Her anger and violence can't defeat,
As forests burn and cities fall,
We can only stand by and watch it all,
The ferocious destructive hostile weather.
Won't be tamed by man, now or ever.

Patricia Barrett

CHRISTMAS ALONE

The shops are full of Christmas goodies;
Bright colours, glitter, music, noise,
Excited children choosing presents
Money going down the drain.

But I don't need this interruption
To my life, lived all alone.
What use is turkey, Christmas pudding?
Only money down the drain.

Janice Hosking

THOUGHTS FOR THE SEASON (LONELINESS)

The first season,
The very first season
I was a child
The weather was sunny.

The second season,
I was a person
A person with colleagues
A person with family and friends
The weather was warm.

The third season struck
My family departed
My health departed
I departed
The weather was icy.

The fourth season is here
I am a grandmother
My daughter is my friend
Relationship's altered.

How to adjust?
To drift like the tide?
Or fight to be heard
To be understood

The weather is cool but improving.

Kay Harding

ONE EARLY SUMMER RECALLED

After tea we usually played in a meadow
Not too far from the farm, far enough not to be seen.
In the stream we looked for darting minnows and built dams.
Watched rabbits, and once on a rock saw an adder.
Meanwhile, eyeing us were two busy nest building birds,
Did their instinct tell them that our presence was no threat?

The hedge sparrows home camouflaged inside the blackthorn.
Soon five bright blue eggs were laid, then every evening
Wondered if they had been hatched, listening for new sounds.
Quietly we approached the hedge, raucous calls thrilled us.
Gaping beaks and orange throats needing constant feeding
Both parents busy again flying off for insects.

Mary E Beale

KILBRONEY

Crooked trees that hang aside
Winding paths that creep and hide
And play a game with our eyes
Mountain water running cold flowing over
Pebbles old filtered clear and sparkling bright
Lying in pools that catch the light
Damp dank woody smell that clears the mind
And makes us feel alive
Soft pine upon the gravel loose
Where walkers' feet do crunch and cling
To soles of souls in boots
Autumn showers of golden leaves
That flutter round and round and down
To lie in wait in heaps so great for man
And beast to scatter round and round
Morning mist swirls soft between the tallest trees
And wets the face and wets the hands of those
That breathe upon the conquered pad and
Breathless bending gasp at the heart of Rostrevor
The standing stone since time began watching
Pilgrims come and climb and stare
And touch by hand this wondrous weathered rock
That is Kilbroney
Fiddlers Green below so clean and single lines
For paths do run between the forest floor
Where acorns lie and squirrels ply their trade
For winter's coming chore
Heather bloomed and growing wild beside the turf
Holes long-since died
And holly trees and rowans small that
Fight for space in nature's mall

Slieve Martin looms through rolling white and
Beckons come and view and sit awhile
And drink the fresh cold air light
And pick a point and point and even argue
Through rose red cheeks that speak forever of Kilbroney.

Michael P Kelly

SECRET TREASURES

The summer skies are fading, moving over to welcome autumn's days.
Memories of holidays and far off places drift away into a distant haze.
The once green leaves have blended into deep reds and golden browns.
Clinging desperately to their branches until finally they tumble down.
The harvest season is all over, the fields are empty of their fare.
With hills no longer lush and green the country scene looks bare.
Ducks are leaving in their groups like great arrows across the skies.
Flying off in search of winter warmth as the heat of summer gently dies.
The cloak of darkness draws in early, the nights seem so very long,
The dawns are breaking later now and the morning chorus is all gone.
The tell tale signs of winter are knocking loudly at the door.
The strength of summer's fight will not restrain it for ever more.
The summer sun has slipped away, disappeared until spring next year,
Only to be replaced by rain and winds and misty days
until the snow is here.
As winter creeps in all around us Christmas lingers in the wings
Tell tale signs are beginning to show, shops filled with beautiful things.
Autumn walks hold extra joys; don't you remember kicking leaves?
As children eagerly await the fall from the great horse chestnut trees.
As decades and centuries pass us by the conker game hold its pleasures
And like all the seasons in the year autumn holds its secret treasures.

Zenda Cooper

THREE SHADES OF AUTUMN

Autumn glows golden even without the sun.
On dark days when a steely sky meets mist or rain,
Still the burnished bushes and trees brighten
And shed a shimmering carpet to swell and shift.

When the sky lightens to gentle silver behind
An ever changing pattern of white and grey,
Then remaining greens in leaves and grass gleam,
A spectrum of eerily emerald shades against the russets.

But when the sky is blue and light pours down,
All strangeness goes and summer seems recaptured,
Caught trying to escape, laughing, still here,
Throwing brightness in the face of her own death.

Chris Sanderson

AUTUMN

September sun fades to autumn sky
Autumn weather seasons change
time passing, colours turning,
green to red and gold.

Autumn leaves fall shedding the past
to a new future that will last
trees bare and still
await winter's chill
knowing they will again bloom.

Nature announces the timeless change
to herald in a new season
to lose but to gain
perhaps through sadness, perhaps through pain
there is a wisdom to learn
and a maturity to lay claim.

Spring to summer
autumn to winter
a time to blossom
a time to fade and wither
a spring like a birth
to replenish the earth
a summer to live a life
to love, to give
an autumn to mature, to season
with time
A life to unfold with wisdom, with reason
a winter to lay to rest the human breast.

Welcome autumn as though summertime
welcome autumn as the season sublime
where life will shed the leaves of experience
that is yours, that is mine
to begin to understand the reason for a season
where a secret flower will blossom and reveal from nature
an insight, a wisdom, a season divine.

David Shannon Cockburn

WHEN HEAVEN CRY

Waking out of a restful sleep
Looking forward to a glorious day
I hear the gentle thudding of heaven's tears
Beating against my windowpanes.

I peep out of my window
Only to see the sky clouded up
The day looking grey and moody
Without the promise of sunshine in sight.

Oh! Why does heaven cry
Casting greyness upon nature
Blanketing me with her mood
And not smile the bright rays of sunlight?

Though when heaven cry
The earth is joyous
For to her it is a blessing
She absorbs in his tears.

Knowing the union will bring forth
To birth all that nature needs
For nature basks in his tears
It is the oil that wheels her circles.

I will not bow my head in gloom
Behind the dark clouds is a silver lining
I will look up to see the sunshine when it peeps
And watch out for the rainbow!

Jennifer Abdulazeez

LIFE CYCLE

Spring it is acoming,
You can feel it in the air,
The sun is feeling warmer now,
Birds sing without a care.

Green shoots are ashowing,
On the bushes and the trees.
You can hear the buzzing
Of the wondrous little bees.

Life is starting its cycle,
As it does each year.
The birthing of the animals,
Like the little deer.

Life will be so busy,
Busy the whole year through.
The feeding of the little ones,
To make them able too . . .
Do the same as mum and dad,
Who the whole year through,
Work and work to bring up
Their own little brood!

CDG

MY AUTUMN

Spring;
Buds on the trees.
Fresh growth all around.
I blossomed once.

Summer;
The time of my youth.
Tasting, sampling.
I was ripe once.

Autumn;
Time has slipped by.
Thoughtful, more mellow.
I carry more fruit.

Winter;
The time it will come.
My body will fade.
I'll leave fresh seed.

Ann

TO AUTUMN WHEREVER YOU MAY FIND HER

Through translucent haze
A watery sun
Spills papery beams on woodland dell
While fairy rings with dewy glaze
Greet blackbirds song and last bluebell
From leafy gown to leafy mat
Works silently the green to quell
As yellow seeps and colours drown
In autumn's wistful magic spell
As russets reel and orange flame dance
Wild, carefree windage, winding knell
As summer fades and amber stalks
The mellow, tranquil scene to sell.

Carol Fisher

LONDON'S TRAMP

In the midst of autumn I write these words,
Of how seasons come, seasons go - like visions loosely blurred.
The wind is howling, leaves lick up the legs of the tramp on the floor
It's the cruellest of seasons, but winter's to come - with its bitterly cold
days in store.

Winter's arrived - I toss him some coins, the leaves have all rotted
away.
It's an icy morning - just another damned fortune in his sorry excuse for
a day.
I pass by that evening - a mass of paper covers his frozen limbs,
Then what a contrast as I reach the station - the fortunates singing their
hymns.

Christmas soon came and soon went. I go on my way back to work now
the welcomed break is over.
March so soon arrives and the blossom appears - the poor man emerges
from covers.

Spring bids farewell, summer holidays next . . . I don't imagine him
going away, so the seasons come and the seasons go but the tramp
always does stay.

Amanda E Hall

SUMMER

Warm and hazy
Soft and lazy
Summer's here
Once more -
Days are longer
Nights are shorter
Parklands blooming
Trees so shading
Pools streaming
Drinks cooling
Soaking the heat
Tanning a treat
Bikini's bursting
Always thirsting
Grass drying
Children crying
Ice cream vans chiming
Mother's tiring
Peaceful evening
So soothing
For blistered backs
Sleep comes slowly.

Anne Harvey

WINTER'S REPRIEVE

Suddenly, I beheld the spring
Caught in the glory of the morn,
Embedded in a meadow,
Breathing mists unto the dawn.

My heart caught with the suns,
That shone amid the grass,
Buttercup and meadowsweet, were
Galaxies of stars.

Beyond, the darkling river
Told secrets to the trees
As they leaned far down and listened
To all its mysteries.

Oh, spring was here for sure as
Flowers breathed that mist
Reflecting back the sun
As each of them it kissed.

I saw it in the river
And in the trees beside
Their new lush green sleeves rustling
As the birds within them cried.

Rabbits playing in the dew
And crows and thrushes wheeling.
Everywhere so busy
Sends all one's senses reeling.

Behold the blossom o'er my head
Behold the chestnut royal
Flowering cones pink, white and red
Upon the rich live soil.

Glory birds, glory trees!
Scenes and sounds like wine.
Glory in the air,
In oak, and ash and pine.

This is what we ached for
In the long dark days just gone.
This is what we dared not dream
When winter seemed so long

But suddenly it's truly here
Like a blessing or reprieve
And everything is yours and mine
And there is no time to grieve.

W M Francis

A Blanket Of Winter

Dark nights closing in,
A blanket of winter.
Heavy clouds all around.
Trees whisper in the wind.
Leaves chase your feet.
Wrapped up warm
Lonely times drift in,
Days to catch up.
Nights to spend in thought.
Safe inside your home.
Open and shut windows of time.
Dazed from inwards.
Traffic passing by,
Shoes upon people's feet.
Hurry, quickly turning corners.
Rushing about sheltering under cover.
Demands of life taping away at you.
Looking out from the window,
Watching
Howling winds stir,
Paper floating like kites.
Snatching winds steal
Hats and scarves.
Those long hours become short.
Night is near draw the curtains,
Sit down feel every day blues
Rush away winter holds your time,
Soft music brings warmth to you,
Upon these winter nights.

Sharron Hollingsworth

JOY OF SUMMER

As far as naked eyes can see
Cornfields stretch forth with colours.
God's gift to man for faithfulness,
A legacy of flowers.

Frail plumes of graceful blossoms
Sway softly in the breeze.
Brown butterflies with folded wings
Suck sweetness deep with ease.

Sweet vernal grass wafts fragrance
Of freshly new mown hay.
While vibrant crimson poppies
Remember by - gone days.

Tall quaking grasses tremble
When beetles scurry through.
In search of golden treasure
That lie in cornflowers blue.

Glossy ox - eyed daisies
Nod idly in the sun.
They watch the bees yield honey
From nectar easily won.

The warm winds blow in summer,
While cornfields ripen gold.
And Ceres smiles resplendent
Joy for her harvest home.

Jan Caswell

SWEET BRYONY

Sweet bryony,
White virgin flower,
Trembling in the wind
You seek his strength,
Entwining limb on limb
For life's support.
You wait the season
To repay the debt -
Garlanding your beloved
When his prime is past.
Scarlet and rich
The fruit you bear
And in profusion
You deck him,
An autumn hedgerow
Now festive
With borrowed beauty.
So will a woman
Endow her man,
His children's children
The harvest of summer,
When the sap was strong
His leaf green,
And he support
And comfort to his own.

Anna Jones

SPRING WEDDING

Oh, marry not in June but wed in May,
When countryside is decked in bride's array:
The hedgerow wears a gown of ivory lace;
And hawthorn blossom transforms every place
With drifts and white cascades on perfumed air
In floral art displays beyond compare.
Horse chestnut candles light green colonnade
Where vaulted tracery gives leafy shade;
The blackbird pipes an anthem sweet and clear
To celebrate this joyful time of year;
Pink petals from the April blossoms past
Are scattered like confetti in her path;
Delicate *lady's smock*, her bridesmaids shy
In palest tint of mauve, tremble and sigh
As radiant bridal May glides softly by.

Valerie Gough

MOTHER NATURE

The lush, green grass quivers in the gentle breeze,
The flowers bob their lazy heads.
Animals lie sprawled to soak up the sun,
The trees whisper that summer has come.

Mother Nature wears her wedding gown,
All her beauty at its peak,
Many look on in silent awe,
Eyes consuming, wanting more.

Inspiring, enticing, enchanting is she,
Astounds, overwhelms and impresses no end,
A paintbrush appears or maybe a pen,
In an attempt to capture this magnificent gem.

The robe she wears is composed of flowers,
An affinity of petals gathers as ruffles,
Her sky of pastel peach and rosy red,
Engulf her splendour and create a cosy bed.

Our eternal Mother grows heavy with sleep,
The sun slowly slips under slumbers' steadfast strength,
Soon darkness enshrouds the earth,
Patiently all await nature's rebirth.

Lauren Pritchard-Gordon

THE MEADOWS IN SPRING

I wandered through the meadows on a lovely sunny day
Came across a lazing fox who quickly ran away.
I saw some pretty squirrels running up and down a tree
They stopped and froze like statues as soon as they saw me.

I watched a prickly hedgehog roll up tightly in a ball
And spied a little field mouse hiding in a broken wall.
I stood and watched the sparrows pecking busily away
Heard a robin redbreast singing saw a wagtail and a jay.

Nearby on a riverbank a frog croaked noisily
Joined with the chorus of the birds and the buzzing of a bee.
Swans were swimming on the lake feathers gleaming white
The little cygnets followed they were such a pretty sight.

Leaves were showing on the trees hedgerows a bright new green
And peeping through old foliage bluebells could just be seen.
The meadows are so pretty in summer, winter and fall
But after a long winter, springtime is best of all.

Mary Millar

NATURE'S MIRACLE

As the years come and the years go
Trees and flowers thrive and grow
A garden gives us so much pleasure
Time to pause with thoughts of leisure.

Butterflies hover on the wing
Dawn chorus of birds that sing
Multi-coloured flowers a sight to behold
A warm summer's day before winter's cold.

Hollyhocks, primroses, sweet scented thyme
Clematis and sunflowers in their prime
Lupins, forget-me-nots, London pride
Honeysuckle, foxgloves, side by side.

Tall delphiniums of azure blue
A sculptured shape of an elegant yew
Heady perfume of roses in the breeze
Gentle swaying of surrounding trees.

Clusters of daisies, poppy's and mint
Changing colours of autumn's hint
Carried by wind, seeds dropped on earth
Nature's act to give re-birth.

A New Year, a New Century awaits us all
Ahead lies winter, spring, summer and fall
Trees and flowers thrive and grow
As the years come and the years go.

Brenda M Hadley

ROBIN

Sprinkle, sprinkle,
Little snowflake,
White and feathery loose.

Sprinkle, sprinkle,
Little snowflake,
Mother Nature's plucking her goose.

Sprinkle, sprinkle,
Little snowflake,
Mister Robin dry your eye.

Sprinkle, sprinkle,
Little snowflake,

You don't understand:
We're all under God's protective hand
And I
Am just as mesmerised as you
By God's magic wonderland so white, so new.

Ken Round

THROUGH THE SEASONS

Spring returns bringing new life,
Bulbs twist forth from winter's sleep,
Feeble helpless like a newborn babe.
Summer comes with stronger sun
Longer days, gardens in colourful array.
Lush green lawns speckled with daisies,
Where children play contentedly.

Autumn with spectacular golden glow
Crispness of fallen wilted leaves
Celebrating in a merry dance
Displaying a carnival of colour and
Fragrance, patiently awaiting winter's
Chill, when white blanket covers hill and dale.
Robin and blackbird chirp in search of food.
Icicles fringe the eves, trees stark
Exposed to the world without a shred of foliage.
Like the seasons of life when spring, summer, autumn
Have passed, winter whispers in chilling
Tones 'Come home,' life's beauty
Revealed with a glimpse through the seasons.

Frances Gibson

BLOOMING MARVELLOUS

Come and see my garden
It's the place to be
Flowers bloom with fine delight
Cheerful and free
Sea winds blow, with salted air
Plant life lives
While others share
The ground, earth's substance
From within
While some plants die
Others begin
Twelve seasons come
And then they go
Some grow up
While others no!
They die before they have a chance
Like a Knight in armour
Parading his lance
He attacks on horseback from afar
I the gardener, get help from a jaw
A can, a spray, whatever will help
As long as it kills the bug
Does it matter, it yelps?
I care for life and nature to
Crawling bugs are fine
As long as there on your flowers
But never on mine . . .

Les J Croft

SEPTEMBER 1951

The speckled starlings brought it back to me,
Clicking, chuckling, great flocks swinging down,
That first autumn in the countryside,
When all I'd known was autumn in the town.

I'd loved the autumn in the busy town,
Going home from school across the park,
To scuffle in the crackling, fallen leaves
As street lamps glimmered in the creeping dark.

Behind the silhouetted chimney pots
The sunset flared across the evening sky,
A final burst of red and yellow flame,
While sooty starlings watched the daylight die.

But, oh! That autumn in the countryside!
Huge clouds of starlings flew across the Weald!
With rhythmic rustling of a thousand wings
They swooped and dived upon the stubbly field.

Rolling through the village on their way
To Kentish hop yards where the vines grew high
Came caravans, by stolid horses pulled,
And cheerful gypsies stopped, to sell and buy.

We gathered fruit with fingers purple stained
In green scented, gentle autumn days.
We foraged in the woods for fallen boughs
To give our winter fires a cheerful blaze.

At night we watched the glorious harvest moon
Clothe the fields with light, and haunting shade.
And heard the soft-winged owl make quivering call.
Oh! How that autumn all its wealth displayed!

Margaret Ballard

FOREVER SUMMER

As the seasons come and go
And spring's bright leaves now autumn cast
The time that once did linger long
Now rushes by so fast.

I look back and see Marilyn,
Diana and Monaco's Grace
Then turning to the mirror see
My old and wrinkled face.

And I wonder if Fate was merciful
By sparing them old age?
For they would find it oh, so hard
As time flicked on each page.

But now their beauty will live on
In poems, lyrics to be sung
And, unlike us, as seasons pass
They'll stay for ever young.

Mary Jennings

AUTUMN PORTENTS

It is still summer.
September hasn't flown.
There's promise yet of roses!
Warm days, brightness, to gather in
The harvest of the heart.
For though October beckons
With growing threat of cold,
The shield within the soul,
Prepared from crops of sun,
Remains intact - undaunted
As honest thought. Dispel
Dull portent's woe and dwell
In summer's afterglow.

Jack Conway

WINTER JOY
(For my beautiful daughter Carrie)

When all the shadows lengthen deep,
And night from day doth sudden leap
The silver beams from moon do shine,
As stars appear in the sky so fine.

When frost on windows makes its lace,
As across this land chill wind doth race,
The leaves have fallen from the tree
And branches bare are all we see.

When snow falls soft from leaden sky,
In drifts deep and white doth it lie.
Here in the hearth home fires roar,
Within me then do spirits soar.

When at day's end you are with me,
Soft in your eyes the love I see.
As I lie snug within your arms
Safe from all of winter's harms.

'Tis then I wish for you to stay,
To love me in your special way,
For then I know you love me so
And you from me will never go.

Anthea C Payne

NOVEMBER

There is a melancholy in the air
raindrops too and winds are sighing.
Petals falling, flowers dying,
leaves in heaps about my feet are lying.
In mourning for his summer song,
his saffron beak now silent,
a blackbird lone and brooding,
sits perched on a twig
in a leafless tree.
The mountain stark is darkening.
Clouds descending, peaks lost to view.
Grey mists swirling, stealthily unfolding
that which lays before it is consumed.
The swallows have all gone now.
They have flown to warmer climes.
Their anxious voice I witnessed
and their restless flight,
as they soared and gathered
on the telephone lines.

Diane Lavery

CHANGING SCENE

Will you look now if I show you, will you listen if I talk
As I take you on a journey to see the treasures as we walk.
We may travel ever northwards where air is pure and clear,
As summer turns to autumn with the passing of the year.

As evening shadows lengthen and trees now turn to gold,
The ever-changing story of seasons now unfold,
Woodlands shed their summer garb and lose the verdant green,
How beautiful the russet shades beside a mountain stream.

The early frosts of autumn, the chill now of the breeze,
A carpet in the forest of crisp and withered leaves,
Nature casts its magic spell, free for all to see,
The beauty of the countryside is there for you and me.

Fruitful now the hedgerows, rowan berries bright,
Brown the hillside bracken bathed in evening's light,
Waves of mist caressing distant silent bens,
Far off cries of wildlife echoes in the glens.

Alister H Thomson

TWELFTH NIGHT

And so is the Twelfth Night already come -
    Christmas season is almost done!
Cards, tinsel - candles - all are gone -
    And into the New Year we *must* move on!

How quickly was the season spent -
    How loud and long the laughter -
Shrieks of delight, and hearty chuckles
    Washed down turkey, 'Criggy' pudding *and*
                           fresh choc truffles!

But now, just the wind stirs the dingle-bells gently -
    'Echoes' of past join with future 'aspiring'
As each faint breath sighs 'Goodbye' and 'Hello' -
    Memories swirl round us - above and below -

Faint heraldic voices, distant - repeating,
    Like the white surf's ebb and flow, ever
Thus singing:
    'Gloria in excelsis deo!'
    'Gloria in excelsis deo!'
    'Shalom! Shalom! Shalom!'

Mary McCaig

THE SEASONS

Spring brings a new beginning - our hopes and aspirations to
                             be achieved,
Our outlook so crisp and fresh, daffodil gold our aim's not to
                             be deceived.
The sun in transition as it opens one eye and gives a half smile
And if we toil we'll succeed - go on, do not wait a while.

Summer with spring's promise smiles and grins and we are now
                             fully alive,
The seeds sewn are fruit trees now and Mary has become Dean's
                             June bride.
The flowers are abundant and we picnic on the lawn,
We don't wish to go inside but work and play hard until the dawn.

Autumn, that tranquil time that says that we must prepare ourselves
                             for life indoors.
We sweep the fallen leaves and those missed we retrieve from
                    underneath the benches crawling on all fours.
The birds' nests hidden before are now open to predators but they
                    have luckily now left our shores,
And as the chill sets in we all have to lock our doors.

Winter's cold, icy and chilling to the bones sees us sitting by the
                             log fires.
Father looks a treat in the plush, red velvet outfit of Santa Claus, one
                of the many items from the fun shop which he hires,
And in church the Christmas bells ring out, 'Ding, dong! Ding, dong!'
A backing sound for the choir as they sing and make merriment in
                         wonderful song.

Margaret Andrews

AUTUMN

I want to hold this moment now and forever;
Remember it in the long winter months ahead.
See in my mind the great rolling Moor
Covered in gold-brown bracken,
And the distant Tors, their granite boulders
Glinting in the midday sun.
Recall the sounds of buzzards mewing overhead
In the high blue sky, and scudding clouds
Cast dappled shadows on the earth below,
Blown by the south-west winds
Which shake the browning leaves remaining on the boughs.
See the bright red berries of the rowan trees,
Glowing like jewels upon a leaf-stripped branch.
Hear the river rushing onwards to the sea,
Cascading over boulders, bubbling over stones,
Eddying and swirling - clear and brown with peat,
Catching the autumn sunlight - never still.
Hear the rustle of leaves as I walk through the wood,
And the damp, dark smell.
See the sunlight shining through the trees;
Holding a green-brown acorn in my hand.
Feel the warmth of the sun on my face,
The stillness and the peace.
Let me remember the beauty around me.
Autumn on Dartmoor on a sunlit day.

Ann Linney

SOMETHING FOUND - A SENSE OF THE DIVINE

You walk with me in the garden
In the warmth of a summer day
You are there in the park with the children
As I watch them at their play.

> When I lift my face to the heavens
> And feel a refreshing breeze
> And here as I pass beneath them
> The blackbirds in the trees.

In the roar of the passing traffic
In the hurrying busy feet
As I do my morning errands
Along a dusty, car-lined street

> As man-made things hurtle round me
> And I start to feel afraid
> I look at the wonders of nature
> And find all the beauty You've made.

Irene Igbinedion

AUTUMN MAGIC

The autumn wind of wisdom blows
How does it know?

Inside planetary prickly sphere
The conker is ready to appear
Shining brown, perfection knows
The wind will blow
And the wind knows.

Brown, golden, russet leaves
Await the autumn breeze
They are clinging so ready to fall
They know the wind will blow
And the wind knows.

Children look to the ground
Where leaves and twigs are found
To build their bonfires high
Children know the wind will blow
And the wind knows.

The autumn wind of wisdom blows
How does it know?

Mary Farrant

WINTER

Deep in the midst of winter's pall
Of cruel frost and petulant storm
So distant now the autumn fall
Sullen, yet unselfishly forlorn.

Shrill winds that blast and howl and scream
That chastise the pallid ground
They ship the sanctimonious cross
And wear the gargoyle's frown.

So hurtful now the bullet-like rain
Knife-edged, and of torrid mood
That swells the river and numbs the face
Of objects that it cannot move.

From cheerless sky through air now still
Falls snow genteel and light
It gracefully settles, its flakes like petals
Uniform, and apple blossom white.

With sharpened tooth and savage bite
The bitter frost doth seek
To petrify Mother Earth's fragile skin
And claw her underneath.

A R Frape

YEN FOR SUMMER

Expansive as summer-sweet sands
when the tide is out and remote
is new zest with fervent demands
for freedom to fly and to float
uncaring, unsullied by storm,
limited lighting, tepid rain.
Shall forthcoming summer be warm?
Shall I feel like singing again?
Colours of August and July
re-awake appreciation?
Dear Lord, when sombre winter's by
shall arrive that same elation?
Like blissful child with daisy-chain,
upon some fantasizing spree
shall I discover gods ordain
a summer of rapture for me?
I visualise birds on a frieze
of scintillating fresh design
soon spread across the moody seas,
a wild anticipation of mine;
they welcome May inveigle June,
honeying changing air with song.
Shall dreams don reality soon?
Still purple shadows hover long.
Promise me a race into blue
and rosy shifts of space and hour
when life emancipated, new
shall flourish like refurbished flower.

Ruth Daviat

AUTUMN BREEZE

I am resting on the window seat,

Looking at the montbretia's leaves,
They are dancing in the breeze,
Performing the twist and the excuse-me,
First from the left, then from the right,
Bending forward and to the side,
Lifting up their slender leaves,
Moving them in all directions with ease.

This gentle breeze is Nature's music,
But dancing is a desired art expression,
Where every movement is full of grace,
The beauty provided in this natural place.
So, at this great moment in time
The everlasting impression is recorded in my mind.

Heavy showers with short spells of sunshine,
Reminding us the summer is receding
Leaves are changing from green to gold and to red,
Providing the ground with a glorious blanket.
Everything is still growing fast
Producing seeds and crops to summer's last.

The glorious autumn is upon us too fast.

Milly Saunders

WINTER JUST GONE

My fingers were cold to the touch,
The chimney needed freeing from soot
So I dared not light a fire, and
The floor was slippery underfoot.

Cups of hot tea grew quickly cold
And the butter from the fridge was hard.
Peeling veg in icy water
Meant enjoyment of cooking was marred.

A walk down to the paper shop
Meant putting on scarf and woolly hat.
The dog wasn't eager to go -
Nothing could move him from where he sat.

How quickly he moved back in June
Along the brightly lit city streets.
When summer has returned once more
We both might move from our comfy seats.

Barbara Pearce

THE SEASONS MUST

Spring ephemeral, bursting forth
its thrusting life, anew
as doth the slumb'ring earthly seed
its challenge, yearly due.

Summer, languid, sultry, hot
early morning dewy start
evenings drifting, balmy haze
these halcyon days, so soon depart.

Soon autumn's mellow presence beckons
its muted, coloured, subdued cloak
of bonfires, wood smoke, chestnuts polish
the falling leaves of ash and oak.

Now cold and ice, in harshness rules
as winter grips, so crystalline
to subjugate, this fragile earth
this battle, old as time.

As seasons follow
seasons must
a cycle everlasting
for man a reason to survive
a just state, for the asking.

Robert Dover

WHEN SORROWS COME

We wonder why it has to be
When sorrows come along our way
The horizons of the morrow
Turn from gold to grey.

All the lovely things we dreamed
Have vanished overnight
Looking out along the road
We seem no gleam of light.

Where then can we look for hope
To break the dark despair
When the cross of our affliction
Seems too hard to bear.

Where can we turn
For consolation and relief
We find blame to ease the heart
And heal the wounds of grief.

Only in the knowledge
That all things are transient
Nothing in this changing world
Is fixed or permanent.

It is but the shadow
Of the great reality
A place is preparation
For a life that is to be.

D Sheasby

SPRING'S MAGIC SPELL

I am enjoying my early morning walk,
The tangy, sharp freshness of the air fills my head like wine.
I am aware of the wonder of this new day's birth.
The birds are so busy building nests,
Their excited chatter fills the air,
I listen to a blackbird's sparkling song
The notes are clear and sweet, they linger in the golden air.
Suddenly her song is interrupted.
The harsh, complaining cries of a crow,
The magic of the morning lost to him.
I see the bright new leaves sprouting forth,
Giving the tall trees a delightful, lacy look.
Beneath, the bluebells spread their colourful carpet.
I stand beneath an almond tree in full bloom
I gaze up into its powder-puff clusters,
Lost in its glorious splendour.
I am encircled by a high, pink parasol.
A soft breeze gently breathes on the perfect, tiny flowers,
Whispering, 'How beautiful you are!'
I am completely enchanted by it all.
Then I sigh, a little sadness touches my heart,
I have arrived at work!

Molly M Hamilton

COMPANIONS THREE

The moon through the window peeped
And saw an elderly lady fast asleep.
Firelight danced upon her white hair
As she dozed in her comfy chair.

Her collie dog lay by her feet,
Snoring and grunting in his sleep.
The tabby cat curled up on her knee,
Contented they dozed, the sleepy three.

The old woman's mouth gaped open wide
As she napped by the fireside.
The table was laid with teacup, saucer and plate,
Ready for supper at half-past eight.

The three companions slept on,
Oblivious of the moon as it shone.
They looked snug on a cold winter's night,
Bathed in the glow of the firelight.

Maj Macaulay

THOUGHTS OF AUTUMN

From our window I can see
Woods and hills where field and tree
Wear their autumn livery.
Slowly autumn fires die
Till the grey November's sky
Tells us winter days are nigh.
Soon the nights more frosty grow
In the night sky planets glow
Marvelled at by us below.
Clouds like towers silent fly
Changing patterns in the sky
Glowing red with sunset's dye.
Autumn is my favourite season,
I was born then, that's the reason.

Margaret Baguley

SPRINGTIME

O beautiful sun!
Part of almighty creation,
warming the earth to life
from months of cold and rain.
Breaking the clogged wet soil
to handfuls of friable tilth;
starting the seedlings springing,
pushing their tiny heads
into the morning air,
to see if the day is fair.
And oh, the sun is warm
as we dress the garden for spring.

O beautiful sun!
Melting the last of the snow
from forgotten combes
and the cold hollow of hills,
where winter's chills
linger too long.
All around me is singing:
all round me the song
of life breaking through,
beginning anew
to make food for the hungry
across the earth;
creation's rebirth.
Praise God for the sun!

D Morcom

THE JOY OF SPRING

The grass grows green
The trees grow tall,
The ivy creeps on yonder wall.
The blossoms bloom,
The flowers grow,
The birds sing softly as they go.
Spring is here!
The sun begins to rear her head,
New lives break through their garden bed
The earth till now so calm and still
Sends up to us the daffodil.
In the fields new lambs at play,
The air perfumed with new-mown hay.
New life in abundance
A gift from above,
Nurturing all with God's blessed love.
What a special season, Lord,
To us you slowly bring.
How good it feels to share with you
Your beauty
We call spring.

Rita Dilks

THOUGHTS FOR THE SEASON

Mild summer
mild winter
keeps me cool and calm
in every moment
every day's kaleidoscopic
life's livings.

It even inspires me to write
otherwise
I am tortured
I am tormented
here and there
now and then
since I developed schizophrenia
as an adult person
suddenly, instantly,
autumn and spring
have their own charms.
One with flowers, birds,
the other foretelling of bloom
coming on doorstep knocking
and inviting to life.

Ghazanfer Eqbal

WHAT'S HAPPENED TO THE SEASONS?

Has Nature's paintbrush lost its bristles?
There's no colour left for the thistles
Heads of purple, leaves of green
A prettier emblem yet to be seen.
Spring has lost its growing flowers,
No more yellow, pink or blue colours.
No trees that have their leaves for long
The seasons seem all lost or gone
Global warming's to blame for this.
Summer comes but no bright sun
Rain pours down, we're all forlorn,
Holidays become such disasters
With lots of tornadoes, hurricanes and earthquakes,
We've spent a fortune rebuilding the mess.
Global warming's to blame for this.
Autumn leaves are on the ground
Crispy carpets of yellow and brown,
No fresh days to go for walks
It's cold and wet, we'll stay in and talk
No fun rolling about in the leaves,
Global warming's to blame for this.
Winter's just around the corner,
Just hope Nature can warn her
The Christmas story without snow
Wouldn't be the same.
I hope global warming's not at it again!

Dorothy Aplin

THE BIRTH OF DAWN

The dawn is breaking
on this beautiful morn,
the sparrows and the robins are chirping,
sharp cries and groans
are coming from the hills, and the valleys.
Hear the animals in the fields
waking and rubbing their heels.

Dawn, oh dawn, why give up thy birthright?
Rest awhile, let me sleep on,
it's a beautiful morn,
let me slumber and dream a little longer,
pity me, let me sleep on my friend,
so that my dreams
can continue to roam beyond.

I know that you can be
nice, sweet and charming,
but at times your moods are
bright, fiery, and cruel
like a star with a super jewel
giving light, fire, and life abound,
but please delay your birth, my dawn
because my dreams can no end find.

Oh dawn your powers are truly breaking
I can feel your strength, and fiery glare
these powers are so great and overwhelmed.
Will my dreams have to submerge with them?
Yet I know the night must end, so let your
powerful force come forth in abundance.

The dawn has at last broken
what a manifest!
Are you life's mystery,
or just part of a test?
I know the sun will soon arise
to show you who is best.

Cora Woolcock

WINTER STORM

The sky was bruised
And cried
Like a battered wife.

With a slap it flushed pink
As silver rakes of electricity
Stung the Earth.

Tortured trees and flowers
Grew tired and hopeless
In the dizzying wind.

A canvas of tension hung
Stretched taught over the night,
Booming as thunder bounced off it.

Cars sliced through the rain,
Eager to escape from under
The frown of the storm.

The storm, lashing out,
A temper lost,
A bad mood unleashed
On the soft and pretty face of the Earth.

Jared Pegler

My Garden In December

How frail, how brave the Prunus flowers
Defying wind and rain and showers
To greet me at the gate.
Across the drive and by the door
Mahonia's golden candles
Spread a carpet on the floor.
And did you see the daffodils beneath the tree?
Not yet a host but quite enough to pleasure me.
Walk down the path toward the hedge
And look, yes really look, there by the edge
Amid the withered leaves of yesteryear.
You'll see a Peony sleeping there.
At last the best that there can be
The Snowdrops raise their heads for me
Such hope such joy the tiny flowers can bring
Tread softly for you're treading on my spring.

Judy McEwan

WINTER TWILIGHT

Curls of smoke from the chimney pot rise
Towards a low, cheerless sky.
A pervasive mist softly spreads
Damp air clings to the chest
As I walk towards home in the winter light,
There will be no moon on high tonight
As the blast of the fog-horn intermittently sounds
A warming to fishermen and throughout the town.
Lamps are lit, curtains are drawn,
Shut out the bleakness, keep in the warmth.

Julie Ann Sloan

TIME OF SUMMER

S   ummertime is finally here,
U   nder the trees, birds are there.
M   uttering and murmuring is the
M   ild summer breeze.
E   verywhere you go, you hear a sneeze.
R   adical heat can fulfil one's need.
T   he flowers are out
I   n the meadows and fields.
M   e and my friends shall
E   njoy the blissful whiff.

Charlene Keyes

WINTER

There's so much tension in the air
people shouting everywhere,
gossiping and being rude
with heavy winter attitudes.

Things get broken, people stare,
grinding teeth and pulling hair.
It's so dark and foggy here,
cold winter nights are drawing near,
with icicles and frost around
and slushy snow upon the ground.

But one good thing about this time
is that it's constantly a sign
that after all the lack of order,
there's always Christmas round the corner!

Presents, trees and decorations,
join in all the celebrations!
After dark and winter gloom this will all be coming soon!

Carol singing, present giving,
ceremonies too.
Remembrance in all the ways of things given to you.

So we are glad that no-one's sad about the winter season,
When Christmas comes, we all will be so happy for a reason!

Sarah Williams

MR SUN-MAN

Dear Mr Sun-Man,

Why won't you come out to play?
It's August 12th, you're meant to come out today.
We've missed you, it just hasn't been fun,
We can't have a summer if there isn't a sun.
I know you think we don't appreciate your work,
But since you've gone, Britain's gone berserk.
We do need you, that is a fact,
So come on please, put on your hat.
Now I know you're angry, since that solar eclipse,
Moon didn't mean to block you, she just wanted a kiss.
We came on that Sunday, we didn't know where you were,
Mother Nature didn't show us, so blame it on *her*.
Come on Mr Sun-Man, only three months to go,
After then it'll be winter, we'll be covered in snow.
You can't come in winter, or the Earth will be ice,
So come out today. Wouldn't that be so nice?

Latoya Brobbey

MEDITATIONS OF BLACK AND WHITE

Scrawny branches claw the sky
As the tempestuous Furies fly.
Autumn's bounteous glory fades
To winter's fustian sepia shades.
Denuded woodlands' grandeur gone
Lost their shelter and their song.

Seasons' sculptor shamelessly rapes
The well-loved and familiar shapes.
Contours within a white mantle lost,
Just odd fringes 'mid glistening frost.
Pendular icicles so steadily growing,
Muted streams that are barely flowing.

Where the North-Easterlies blow
Playing with little puffs of snow,
Starched uniforms white statues confine,
Defined designs that are etched in rime.
Strictured within this monochrome,
Only the briefest of sunsets roam.

Enigmatically embracing blackest night
The crystalline evening gown grips tight.
Shades and colours are not allowed
Virginal white the adumbrate shroud.
Perquisite as inventories' Advent' time,
Introvert reflections are frozen in mime.

Yet once again life will resurge,
From pupal dormancy re-emerge.
Colours more vibrant following demise
Will once again delight the eyes.
As Nature again her pallet flings,
And blossoms bloom 'mid beating wings.

H D Hensman

LEAVES EVERY AUTUMN

Leaves make a lovely crispy, crunchy sound.
Whenever I am sad,
I kick leaves so they shuffle around and
dance in the air.
Whenever it rains, they are drowned
and very lifeless.
The colour of the leaves which are bright and bold
are sparkly, spanking gold,
fiery, roaring red,
deep, dark, dull brown and
light, shining yellow.
What marvellous, miraculous colours.

Joanna Morgan (10)

PHEW!

The heatwave is going to continue
Breaking all records the weather forecast says.
Great, how wonderful, the general reaction
But not from me, all I can say is 'Phew!'

Dripping all day, at night a soggy pillow,
Pores overworked, exhaustion, brain gone numb.
Trees, plants and grass in state of dehydration
Brought near to death by that fierce relentless sun.

O for some clouds to relieve the boring blueness
And bring again design and texture to the sky.
Clouds full of rain to be drop by drop delivered
To the parched earth so beauty lives again.

The heat and drought are going to continue
No change for at least another week the forecast says
Hurrah - hurrah, again the loud reaction
But not from me, all I can say again is 'Phew!'

Phyllis Moore

WHICH SEASON IS THE BEST?

Wintertime is dreary with no leaves upon the trees,
No sun shining in the sky and all the waters freeze,
But there is beauty all around if we will only see,
The lovely snowflakes and frost patterns on the naked tree,
It is the time when nature rests, the birds do seldom sing,
But what a difference there will be in the days of spring,
There's beauty in the flowers, the buds begin to form,
The cold wind is replaced by the spring breeze so nice and warm,
Then along comes summer when nature is in full bloom,
Too hot to sleep or walk around, young birds have left their home,
Autumn follows summer, the leaves begin to fall,
Still there's beauty to find which should cheer one and all,
Along comes winter, once again nature takes another rest,
Time for lighting fires and wearing warm clothes is best,
But do not be despondent, enjoy what nature brings,
Praise the Lord for all He sends and let your heart have wings,
We can find plenty to complain about if we feel that way,
But give thanks to the Lord and you will find new blessings
                                        every day,
You may search north and south or to the east or west,
If you look to God you'll never wonder which season is the best.

Stan Gilbert

GOODBYE MY LOVE

Never will I see again
Your dark and twinkling eyes
Never will I hold you
Or hear contented sighs
Never will you look at me
Or hold me in your arms
Never will you cradle me
Or shelter me from harm
Never will I hear your laugh
Or share a joke or two
Never will we just embrace
For you and I are through
You told me that you loved me
Among other things you said
You said we'd be together
It went right to my head
For I believed you in all things
I shouldn't have trusted you
For you've let me down so badly
And my heart is broke in two
For you have re-discovered
That you love your Nina more
She has moved in with you
While I was shown the door
So good luck Dave in all you do
And think of me sometimes kind
I hope you get what you're looking for
I hope you find peace of mind

For I will always love you
I know that it sounds strange
But my feelings are too great
For me to ever change
But if you ever need me
Pick up the phone and call
And I will gladly come to you
Winter, spring, summer or fall.

Virginia Barrasin

FROZEN MOMENT

Nose pressed hard against the windowpane
Breathing cold, feeling winter's pulse.
Virgin blanket cloaks the ground -
Crisp like perfect icing on a cake
Gnarled blue-white fingers hang as branches
                                         from the trees
A creak and moan as sudden strain
Dumps the snowy load upon the ground
Then all is still - no life it seems
As isolating whiteness freezes time.

Turning from the window to the room
The log fire beckons, draws me back
To smugness of a previous time
Inside the womb,
Safe.

Brenda Dove

SNOW

Familiar to our eyes
And yet perpetual wonder
To see the countryside transformed
With glistening, stiffened splendour.

Familiar are grey skies,
But now the earth's illumined
With countless million patterned flakes
Ethereal, unassuming.

How quiet and still it lies,
'Til muddled footsteps spread
And where a patch is undisturbed,
A happy child will tread.

Consideration it defies,
Makes modern man go slow,
So while we pause - appreciate -
The phenomenon of snow.

Joan Novak

UNCONDITIONAL LOVE

My heart is torn in pieces
my tears fall like the rain,
a part of me is dying
will we ever meet again?

I gave you life and taught you
as well as I knew how,
the mistakes I made were many
I can see my errors now.

There never were conditions
when I gave my love to you,
don't tarnish or abuse it
for a mother's love is true.

You've grown into a person
I hardly recognise,
your personality is changing
before my very eyes.

I knew one day you'd leave me
and walk the path of life,
to realise your ambitions
and change from daughter into wife.

You could have done it differently
we could have talked it through,
the only thing I wished for
was a better life for you.

So travel down your chosen road
may happiness be thine,
I will love you for my lifetime
O daughter dear, of mine.

Pamela Brannon

SUMMER UNSEEN

Forgotten is the winter's storm,
The sun upon my face is warm.
Summer spreads its joy around -
Children's laughter - happy sound.
Fragrant scents assail my nose,
Honeysuckle, lilac, rose.
I feel the zephyr's soft caress
And every sense that I possess
Strives to picture in my mind
The summer scene -
For I am blind.

They tell me that the grass is green,
I can't imagine what they mean.
They say the sky above is blue -
What is it like? I wish I knew.
My world is mostly dark and grey
With little change 'twixt night and day.
Colours are a mystery
I'll never solve, for I can't see
But all my other senses say -
'Be happy - it's a summer's day!'

George Woodham

FULL CIRCLE

Night stars shine light
on new-born leaves and buds
cobwebbed with crystal frosts.
As new dawn paints its light
dew drops breathe their kisses,
and build new life within the earth.

> In this light and sun
> new life has awakened.

As night fades and light grows strong
goodness fills the earth.
The battle between good and evil is won,
and darkness no longer looms.

> Star-crossed rainbows dance the samba
> amongst the cotton clouds; life is easy,
> for now.

Autumnal years bring suicide,
a need to hide and shelter.
Colours marred with the reaper's touch
brings fear to all with life.
There are no witnesses,
as one last soldier struggles with atrophy
to keep hold in no-man's land.
part-masked in the mists of eternity.
How long can forever be?

> Fade out . . .

Harsh like steel, the chill cuts deep
and clutches mother nature by the throat.
Winter's song is sung
lead-lined tears of ice fall out,
shelter is scarce and hope is little.

A snow blast holocaust
ends existence for the dying.
The time has come for a change.

Becki Mee

SEASONAL DREAMS

At this time of year I have visions
Of leaving behind my heart
The seasons captures all feelings
Emotional then torn apart.

Aggression reveals new energy
When love and hat collide
The truth you disguise within you
And promises turn into lies.

You can't follow dreams forever
And it's time now to decide
Can we really develop our problems
Without needing to criticise.

Look how far we've come now
Should we throw it all away
Or can we build upon our love
And be together for Christmas Day.

E Snell

SEASONS' CHANGES

Winter days spent in front of fire
As it brings rain, gales and ice-cold snow
Although snowballing can be fun
I definitely like being indoors
Watching as the weather comes and goes

Springtime brings promises of what's to come
As the birds sing their chorus of love
It's the lovers' time to be strolling hand in hand
As the sun shines through the hazy clouds
Everything around you starts coming alive

Summer's months are the best
On goes the shorts and our little tops
As we enjoy the heat, we're full of well being
Watching the flowers sway in the summer breeze
In lush green fields by the river's edge

Autumn brings with it a crisp refreshing air
Bringing a healthy colour to everybody's face
The trees are bare, there's a sprit in the air
As kids play with autumn's leaves on our streets,
Soon we'll be wearing our big coats, as the winter freeze approaches.

Lorraine Saunders

AUTUMN

Is it that time of year again,
I can feel it in the air again,
The leaves are turning brown again,
And now they're falling down again.

Is it that time of year again,
The air is getting cold again,
The frost is coming down again,
And now I'm scraping the car again.

Is it that time of year again,
Time for scarves and gloves again,
Time for socks and boots again,
I'm all wrapped up and warm again.

Is it that time of year again,
It's dark before you know it again,
I'm glad when I'm home and safe again,
In for the night and rest again.

It's that time of year again,
My favourite time of year again,
When Hallowe'en will soon be here again,
And things going bump are the norm again.

It's that time of year again,
Make sure you follow the code again,
Watch from a distance be told again,
Or the opportunity might not arise again.

It's almost his time of year again,
Time for us to be good again,
Spare a thought for those in need again,
And be grateful for what we receive again.

Kerridwen Jeffery

THE LANGUAGE OF DRY LEAVES

Today I heard the dry bells
of winter in the brown leaves
of the oak. A weak orange sun
and a thin icy wind
gave a clue of how things were.

From out there to in here
you can hear that one
speaking in a seamless kind of
language you only have to listen
with every nerve of your intention.

A friend rang and spoke
of feeling strange, something's
in the breast she said and
she needed to be awake.

That's what Buddha said
when they asked him if
he was a god or a man.
He said simply, I am awake.

I am awake too cried the crow
I am always awake
did you see the mud marks
of my feet where I crossed
your path today. I am awake.

And I was awake when I
heard the clanging of the dry
oak leaves. Now it's winter.

Dei Hughes

SUMMER

When summer sunshine gives us joy
And long, light evenings, pleasure,
Let's glory in its beauty,
For it is ours to treasure.

Sparkling streams and still, calm seas,
Blue skies and birdsong too,
Sunsets at the close of day
And flowers of every hue.

Each season has its beauty.
It was created so.
And summer in all its glory
Will nature's secrets show.

H Taylor

CHRISTMAS TIME

Christmas time
Is a time to be jolly
Sprays of mistletoe
And holly
Snow outside
A winter's morn
A time some people feel
Forlorn
Comfort those
This Christmas time
Banish your foes
And love one and all
It's Christmas time
Let's have a ball

Theresa Hartley

WINTRY THOUGHTS

Slow in silver splendour
the late autumn sun ascends
and feathered flock
its westward journey wends,
leaves of brown and twisted yellow
even in their dying numbers
spread a ground floor carpet thick
enough to hide the squirrel's nuts;
the floor above
bare-branched and poignant
with the last few fluttering flags
displays an empty nest,
the cold-eyed feline
casts a fleeting glance,
the pink-tongue flick across her lips
betrays her sour-graped solace
as she settles on the garden wall
while down below
beneath a mound of weed
with plaintive squeal the hedgehog
bids farewell.

Evelyn Leite

FREEDOM

Wandering down life's leafy lanes, drinking in the view,
Pausing to gaze at the abundance of flowers in multi-coloured
Hue along the hedgerows, lush and green, bowing to the
Running stream of water clear and cool, as on and on
It tumbles into waiting pools.

The gifts of sense, nose and ear, and eye, gifts
Of grace from our Lord on high; all tell of His love
So pure, a love that is ours for evermore. The beauty
Of creation, of land and sky, and sea, all given by Him
For us to enjoy, His gifts for you, His gifts to me.

Warm summer sun upon my face, birdsong on the air,
Beneath my feet the soft green grass, and my worries disappear.
Disappear from my heart with each bird call shrill and clear;
Disappear from my mind, dispelling all my fear.
Fear, no more insurmountable, for peace has captured all;
The peace of Him who is my God, my Springtime and my Fall.

Catherine Riley

SPRING IS HERE

Birds are busy with their nests
   flowers are budding all around
Now spring is here and winter gone
   no ice or frost is found

Nature has waved her magic wand
   to show a wondrous scene
The colouring of the early flowers
   now all around are seen

The daffodils and the crocuses
   are seen most everywhere
A blessing after wintertime
   a season without compare

Most people love the springtime
   it seems to set their spirits free
With growth in abundance
   a feast for eyes to see

Lachlan Taylor

WINTER SEEN

Now winter sun adorns the woods and fields,
With strands of saffron light on virgin snow,
Naked trees and solid earth transformed,
Into a soft white wilderness, as though
A cloth of innocence could hide within
Its folds the darkness of malignant sin.

Children, wrapped like dolls, in woollen scarves,
Tumble out to play, their florid cheeks aglow,
While polished skaters glide like shooting stars,
Across the firmament of ice and snow.
But a proud snowman collapses from the heat,
Leaving nothing but his pipe and bare clay feet.

When daylight fades, and bitter cold returns,
The sick and needy struggle hard to cope,
As carol singers fill the frosty air
With half-forgotten words of joy and hope,
Words which echo round the hollow womb of night,
Where flickering lanterns spread celestial light.

While, through church windows, pallid moonlight
Falls on heartless effigies of stone, which now lie
Cold and still, on stone-cold lips which never speak,
And eyes which shed no tears to laugh or cry,
But still, as seasons pass and time ages,
Gaze up in wonder at the changing sky.

A K S Shaw

THE WINTER SEASON

The first fall of winter snow has completely carpeted the ground
Drifting in places during the night, without making any sound
Icicles hang from the roof, snowflake patterns on the windowpane
To venture out in weather like this, would really be insane

This picture postcard view, one can't help but admire
All the more pleasurable by the glow of a blazing fire
The cold northerly wind has fiercely started to blow
Cotton wool like clouds above, probably filled with snow

Pavements are becoming slippery, be careful where you tread
I think I'd like to hibernate, go back to my warm cosy bed
Battling against the elements, really isn't any fun
I'll never complain about the heat, I'd rather have the sun

The weathermen forecast a cold night with skies starting to clear
Temperatures dropping to freezing and conditions will be severe
Roads first thing will be treacherous, so please take extra care
I'm glad I have no work today, I haven't got to go anywhere

With a hazy sunshine gradually, the winter wonderland does thaw
Further problems occurring, with the valleys flooding once more
The weather now is calmer, allowing us to go our different ways
How I long for spring, so we lose these long cold winter days

Linda Brown

BLACK BAGS

Black bags loosen,
caught by the wind
unprotected in the field.
Frayed

edges tear
straw escapes
flies skywards
whirls high and free.

Not fodder, no
mere meal -
in the next field
the sheep watch.

The rain breaks
the wind drops
the straw falls
meets the dirt, trodden

underfoot by hungry sheep
nosing, searching
finding
loose black bags.

Straw.

Anne Gibson

SUMMER REFLECTIONS

Amongst the buttercups she treads,
Her spirits rise with every move.
The languid sun up overhead
    Reflects the golden blooms.
Newly dressed trees with saffron haze
Turn mellow leaves towards the heat,
The wispy fronds of willows laze -
    Inches from the buttercups.

The stream still deep from springtime rain,
Meanders its way noisily -
Over and round rocks, its refrain
    Tinkles by tunefully.
She takes leaves from a laurel bush,
Over the side of a bridge she leans.
Throws them in the stream with a rush -
    Chasing along in teams.

Leaning over the parapet,
She sees her reflection shimmer;
'That's me' she smiled and her gaze met
    Eyes looking up a-glimmer.
The sound of water on its way
Makes her feel the world is so grand,
'Hi,' she waves, 'it's a lovely day.'
    And back waves a silvery hand.

Susan Naile

A SUMMER SONG

The cold, dark winter days
edge into the soft warm
resurrection time of spring
when the returning sun
engenders the annual birth of buds
as the pulsing green blood of the earth
flows through the arteries
of the winter murdered world.

Then summer erupts
and earth becomes
a sacred chalice
filled with the golden solar wine.

Radiant blossoms fall,
petals gently drifting
to the waiting soil
as the unencumbered apples
firm and swell
red, green and golden gifts
from busy dedicated bees . . .

Stephen Gyles

PICTURESQUE AUTUMN

Like a beautiful tapestry
Touched only by nature's hand
Autumn unveils her beauty
Spread across the land
Though roses now begin to fade
And the flowers have grown old
Upon green and rustic landscapes
Tree tops are crowned
With fiery amber
And shiny gold
Vibrant sunsets
Shades of grey mauve
Pink cream and blue
Twilight brings a mist in the air
Daybreak is wet with dew
Conkers hang gleaming brown
Gusty winds bring fragile leaves
Of russet, red and mellow yellow
Spinning, twirling, falling down
Looking at the bronze and gold scenery
Autumn in sunlight
Creates a striking picture to me.

Joan Taylor

LOVE OF A SEASON

I love all the seasons of the year
But especially changeable autumn.
Sometimes a warm, sunny Indian summer
When the leaves suddenly change colour,
Pre-dawn frost forms upon the ground.
I love that extra hour in bed when the clocks change.
The rain, which was elusive in the summer season,
Floods town and country alike.
On the coasts storms break through, bursting piers and low barriers,
Trees shed glorious, auburn leaves which, as they
Float down, are caught by the wind,
Some sodden by the rain while others 'fly' onward,
Blocking drains, roads, railway lines and hedges, forming heaps
                                                    of compost.
The nights grow longer as I glance through the window
Dusk approaches - the leaves have disappeared, leaving stark twigs,
Sturdy, determined boughs creak in the wind,
Darkness has fallen the fire crackles merrily in the grate,
Heralding bed, to listen to the howling wind
With the accompanying autumn noises,
Dreaming of the beautiful autumn colours
That are soft to the eye, warm to the heart.

T B Smith

GODDESS OF THE FIELDS

Crimson poppies how
Bright your petals lie,
Among the yellow cornfield
Growing up so high.

The gentle breeze doth
Blow your pretty heads.
Whilst tiny creatures
Rustle in corn-made beds.

You dance away so
Bright and free, the
Goddess of the fields
You seem to me.

Yet the reaper comes to
Banish you from my eye.
The golden fields no longer,
Your crimson heads to die.

Autumn comes then winter's
Snow, such colours then
To come, so soon to go.

Though I wait for spring's
Warm breeze, oh summer's
Poppy 'tis your crimson
Heads that please.

Beryl Smyter

THOUGHTS OF THE THIRD SEASON

Dew-spangled webs, gossamer spun
Iridescent fronds shimmering, caught by the sun,
Autumnal mists in valleys swirling,
Grandfather's beard white whiskers curling, on
Hedgerows where ripened berries cluster,
Thrushes blackbirds - singing muster
Bloom-covered sloes, hawthorn berries red
Pale-coloured fungi overnight has spread
Misty morning . . . autumn equinox
Reddy-brown leaves camouflages old dog fox
In the orchard wind-fallen apples lie
Attracting insects and foraging magpie
Horse and ploughman together toil
Unhurriedly furrowing rich damp soil
Followed by gulls and blue-black crows
Shrieking, scavenging amongst earth-turned rows
New season colours mellowly appear
Summer ended autumn is here

Val Farrell

SNOW QUEEN

Dour and doleful, she dragged her feet
Over the stretching cat-shaped draught excluder
And into my living room gloom as the central heating crackled.
Then she perched upon my shoulder;
A snow-queen with icicles for fingernails,
Cruel as Cruella de Vil,
Haunting me like Churchill's 'black dog',
Squatting like Philip Larkin's toad, 'Work'.
My attempts at wit and Christmas cheer
Failed to pitchfork her off;
She is here to stay,
Adding her weight to my weary winter day.

William Greig

CLOCKS BACK

It's time to turn the clocks back
For summertime is ending
Autumnal leaves are present,
Their colours gently blending.

Reds, golds, soft browns are drifting
And tumbling day by day,
Carpeting all the pavements
While greens just fade away.

The trees stand tall and naked,
Their branches gnarled and bare
Majestic in their splendour
Autumn reigns just everywhere.

Elizabeth Spencer

MAY MARRIAGE

From each tree thin wisps of vapour,
Curl to greet the morning sky,
But this cool mysterious water,
Is unseen by common eye.
Tuned to sun and turning earth,
Month of May thus gives them birth.

Awakened from a winter's sleep,
Apple-blossom into sight,
Ostrich feathered debutantes,
Cirrus fronds on sky's expanse.
Bridal wreaths for May month's marriage
Of its time and of our passage.

Arthur Hurd

SEASON'S GREETINGS

My garden is a peaceful place
In wintertime when there's no trace
Of bird lime, only orphan ants are seen
(Snow turns everything pristine)

My garden is a tranquil place
In spring when golden daffodils face
South and smile a greeting every day
(A tubful flowered into May)

My garden is a hectic place
In summer when fat slimy slugs trace
Kilroy was here on garden paths
(The beer they had has made them daft)

My garden is a restful place
In autumn when crisp leaves replace
The green, to hide the things I dread
(Slugs, bird lime and mouldy bread).

Betty Lightfoot

FROSTFIRE

There's sparkle on my window
Like the facets of a stone -
All the colours of the rainbow
In that one crystal, alone -
This fabulous crystal garden,
Myriad colours, flowers of spring
Painted by the touch of sunbeams
From the light of faery ring
Dancing o'er my frozen window
With the shadows as they pass,
Burnished reds and guilded yellows
From the fire within the glass . . .
Frozen pearls adorn white cobwebs
In a corner of the pane,
Weaving complicated patterns
From the dew and fallen rain,
Deftly woven by a spider
In the warmth of sunlight glow,
With the silken thread within her
Soft as newly-fallen snow.
Unseen spirits of the morning
Take the sunbeams in their arms
Gather rainbows, crystal flowers, flames,
All vanish with their charms . . .

Gone, the sparkle on my window -
Gone, the fire within the glass -
Gone, this moment'ry enchantment
With the shadows . . . as they pass . . .

Carolyn Smith

SHADOWS OF COMPARISONS

If you would know me
look upon poetic words,
that filled blank pages.
Seasons, compared within my mind.

Bare, the face of winter.
Morose with eerie empty branches,
till snowed upon.
A resting place
to cover their nakedness.

Each season blinding with change.
The strength of spring,
that thrusts its way through darkness,
to lighten imaginations.

Brilliance of summer, clouded over
to rain down Mana,
enables green carpet fields
to widen sparkled reflections.

The colour turn of leaves.
Golds, reds and ambers,
shine tears of departure,
loathing the fate of their future.

Know me.
Read into each line
comparisons that constitute lives.

Leslie Fine

IN THE AUTUMN OF LIFE

In the autumn of life
we begin to shed our greed.
For in the autumn of life
we have more than we need.

In the autumn of life
we shed a lot of tears.
For in the autumn of life
we lose many of our peers.

In the autumn of life
we look back to good times.
For in the autumn of life
we break down so many times.

In the autumn of life
we prepare to take our leave.
For in the autumn of life
we haven't much time to achieve.

Charles Owusu

SEASONAL THOUGHTS

It is again that time of year,
    When everyone hopes to have some cheer.
As time goes by and we get older,
    When winter comes the weather gets colder.

In and out of shops people all try,
    For a special someone a present to buy.
Christmas is a time for loving and giving,
    So hard these days with the high cost of living.

How many will know about the *real* reason,
    That lies behind this festive season.
When that Holy Babe laid in a manger,
    Surrounded by cattle to keep Him from danger.

The stars shone very brightly that night,
    Bringing to us God's great gift of light.
So, let us all join in our thoughts and pray,
    Giving thanks to God for that first Christmas Day.

June F Allum

TANGO

Autumn crept in before we had even noticed.
Black, rain-sodden boughs and the burnt-orange, red-veined leaves
cascading like silk down the iron rail.
The beech a tent of purple and wine-red.
Chill wrapping itself by stealth into our throats and eyes
The stillness of day
The delicate pink trumpets of the rhododendrons a last reflected pool of
light before winter, compact varieties, mistaking October for May.

Heart of my heart I see you in my mind.
Striding out, the leaves crackling under your feet,
Your fall as bright as any summer
The dead heat tinged with the least bite of cold.
You cannot see me lift the pansies - winter flowering mixed,
out of their cardboard husks.
Yellow, purple - blue faces plain and blotched, their damson eyes
reproaching each time I break a stem from the bright blue bags.
But you feel me so you say.
Hugging me to your green coat in Barcelona while the waves
cascade like diamonds below the shore.

When we were young we instigated revolution.
Now we know better.
Make music in the night and dance tangos
Bring the great wave of sound resonating across the orbs of the trees

I hand you two gladioli. When you look at them let them speak
to you of me.

Anna Whyatt

WINTER SUNDAYS

My heart once more is full of despair
I feel as if I'm trapped in a lair,
The love of my life has left me again
Each time he goes he makes it quite plain.
'You know I must - it's a promise I made.'
I know! - His honour can't be mislaid.
It doesn't make me feel any better
As I stand in the rain getting wetter and wetter.
Thirty minutes later and I'm thoroughly chilled
My boots - with rain - already half filled.
Then suddenly the weather clears
And all around me there are cheers.
In spite of itself my heart lifts with pride
And I let myself go and flow with the tide.
I shout, I scream, I jump up and down,
In fact I act just like a clown.
Although a game my love plays for pleasure
Sunday rugby is not my idea of leisure.

Margaret Phillips

AUTUMN

Earlier fades the daylight,
Dawn is bedecked with dew,
Birds swoop and swerve in flight
Ready to leave for countries new.
Leaves get sparse upon the bough,
It's autumn now.

Over far and wide
Harvest has taken place.
Everywhere the countryside
Takes on a winter face,
And the land is under the plough
It's autumn now.

The sun has lost its heat,
Colder become the showers.
Winds are rough when they meet
The last of the summer flowers
Which bend to the ground and bow,
It's autumn now.

Lilian Owen

I REMEMBER . . .

I remember springtime and how things used to be.
Young lambs in the meadows, chickens running free.
Buttercups and daisies growing in the grass
Until pesticides were used and they grew no more alas.

I remember summer and long hot sunny days
Of fragrant smelling roses, no harmful ultra-violet rays.
Sandcastles on the beaches and pretty-coloured shells
Or paddling in the ocean free from sea's polluted swells.

I remember autumn and the beauteous flaming trees.
Misty, dewy mornings before the branches lost their leaves.
The smell of bonfires burning, baked potatoes, apple pies,
Not exhaust fumes; leaded petrol choking up the skies.

I remember winter and rich deep fluffy snows.
Robin redbreast in the garden, Jack Frost nipping at my nose.
Evenings huddled round the fireside, hot mugs of steaming teas
Not damp and muggy city streets and balmy spring-like breeze.

There used to be seasons
There used to be four
One could define them
Now they're separate no more.

Sue Goodman

SEASONS OF HOME

Watching boats sailing by
From my hill top so high
Looking out across the bay
On a warm summer's day

Watching a golden eagle fly
Wishing I could get that high
The top of my Ben is all I can make
Now the autumn winds have started to break

Watching deer wander by
Coming down from the hills close by
Now from the clouds' great height
Falls the snow turning my glen winter-white

Watching the salmon's sudden leap
Seeing lambs through soft grass creep
Looking to see how they find their way
On this bright spring day

Katrina Holland

THE DRIFT OF TIME

Leaves drift,
dancing with rhythm
into whirlwind
pyramids.
Dark secrets of the past,
transforming barren leaves
into lips of time.
Chanting in the breeze,
dancing lives away,
the lives of mortal men.

Patricia Gargan

WINTER BLISS

Stillness of the white, cold winter's brightening light
Glistened around the fringes of my windowpane
Pressing, silently knocking, begging to be let in
Desiring to spread a balmy blanket around me,
Me tucked up in bed, my bedroom roasting like warm toast

Curtains drawn, I lie and stare, snug, smiling,
Watching the morning unfold, nature uncurl
Gloved in by the mountainous bales of snow
Soft and glittering, millions of fairy drops fall
Diamond drops darted on trees, turning into crystallised cones
Watering, my mouth tasted of vanilla, rum-current and mango-
flavoured ice-cream

Stillness of white around evergreen, the holly and the ivy
Clothed in coats of righteousness. It is a humbling sight to behold
I lay and watched, until the falling drops stopped
Quietness, a tranquil bliss shout, echoing loud
From its hardening, hoary, crystal rainbow teeming breast
Begins a softening, trickling stream's flow, uninviting,
Yet inviting as a mother giving suck to her suckling child

Rosetta Stone

ONE WINDY NIGHT

'Oh, let me in,' cried out the wind,
The child ignored its pleas
So it rattled on the windowpanes
And shook the tops of trees

'Do let me in,' it howled
And would not leave the child alone
That had hugged the duvet closer
Hiding from the great unknown

'Let me in!' It threw
The dustbin lid across the lawn
And stomped around the garden
Feeling lonely and forlorn

'You stay out there!' cried out the child
'You moan too much for me'
So, in a huff the wind whirled off
And let the poor child be

Kim Montia

A GARDEN FOR ALL SEASONS

'A garden is a lovesome thing'
When it awakens in the spring
The perfumes of the flowers bring
me joy.

A garden is a peaceful place
With warm sun shining on my face
And God has given me this space
in summer.

A garden is a leafy glade
Of crimson, brown, gold and jade
A multicoloured carpet laid
by autumn.

When the robin comes to sing
And Christmas bells being to ring
A garden is the bleakest thing
God knows!

Sara Newby

To John Keats

Autumn again, John, and October leaves
Rustle in drifts about the cottage doors,
We are grown desolate, the world is dulled
Like a snuffed candle, lifeless without flame.

'Beauty is truth, truth beauty' is it so?
Was that one answer Pilate would not hear?

Something we look for, something we desire,
Take, then, the drug of noise, and try to lull
The fear that strikes when we wake at night alone;
Beyond the shadows, darkness' eyeless leer,
The claws groping upon the window glass.
'The rest is silence,' silent the vaults of death,
A desolation of unbroken silence.

So keep the television chattering.
Switch on the radio, or your CD,
Fill all the space with noise and nattering,
Feel better when you've had a cup of tea!

But the doors will close, the world will fade like a dream,
The light of moon and stars will be darkened then
The silver cord will be loosened, the soul will be free.
What shall I do? And is there no escape
From the awesome gift of immortality?
What do I know on earth? What need to know?

The voice comes clearly through the mist of time,
'Be still, and know that I am God' He said.

Margaret Sproat

WINTERTIME?

Looking out the window, what is there in sight?
All I see are piles of snow, that lay there pearly white
Just like the picture postcards, one sees at Christmas time
Where on those picture postcards, it always looks just fine
But when it's in my garden, and it falls down from the roof
It's nothing but a nuisance, and here I have the proof
For I have been out with the shovel, I have been out with the broom
It will be up to my armpits, if it does not give up soon

I see a little sparrow through my windowpane
He is looking for some food, but his hunt is all in vain
For though he is God's creature, or at least they tell me so
If God so loves this creature why hide his food with snow
Out there in the fields, young lambs have just been born
And now they're in a blizzard, their mother's food is gone
All things on this earth, are for a purpose, so they say
I hope the chap who said it, is out in this snow today

Then looking in the larder, I think oh God no
I find my food is running out, and shopping I must go
Then walking up the High Street, where the snow lay inches deep
I find it is a struggle, to stay upon my feet
The roads were cleared, the traffic flowed, in fact it went at speed
The paths they had not bothered with, I suppose they thought no need
And as the traffic sped along, it threw up all the slush
And us poor souls upon the path, it covered all of us
But with it all I struggled on, then homeward made my way
Where once indoors I just knelt down, I thought that I should pray
For all those passing motorists, that drive without a care
I hope next time they pass this way, they will have more time to spare

Once more I rise up to my feet, and to the window go
My hands and feet are frozen, and my spirits are quite low
Outside the snow is deeper, the garden out of sight
As I make it to your chair, my thoughts are for the night
The wind will blow, the doors will shake, and down will come the snow
Do I like the wintertime? The answer is plain, *no!*

S C Wiggins

DECEMBER

Delicate snowdrops ring today,
White roses and fancy cards
must be on their way.
The coffee stands cold and old.
Snow begins to fall.
Voices fade from the market place.
A Christmas tree now fills the space
where once a flower vase stood.

Tom Clarke

AUTUMN, WINTER, SPRING AND SUMMER

As the autumn comes to the trees, they unfold
Their beautiful mantles made of copper and gold,
Ruby-red berries glinting in the bushes,
Guarded so jealously by blackbirds and thrushes.

But now the winter is drawing nigh
Told by all the heralds in the sky,
With honking geese and the fieldfares rush
To look for food in field and bush.

It is now that nature takes her yearly rest,
This is her holiday, she has done her best.
Just as we are getting used to the winter's cold
A bit of magic starts to unfold.

Silently at first, then with a flurry
Spring has started in such a hurry,
Up through the snow and half-frozen ground
Beautiful flowers now abound.

Snowdrops and crocus, ladies of the spring,
The air is much warmer, and the birds begin to sing.
As the sun begins to climb higher with each passing day
The trill of the curlew tells us it's May.

Now the cuckoo, who has come afar
He is shouting 'Come out, come out, wherever you are,'
It is summertime, be in good cheer,
See the swifts and the swallows, they are also here.

Oh! What a wonderful place this land where we live,
Where Mother Nature has so much to give.
It starts with a smile and ends with a sigh,
Enjoy each season as it passes you by . . .

Brian Ducker

AUTUMNAL TEARS

November wind stripped bare
The willow on the lawn.
Its weeping branches
Shed
  Like
    Tears
      Their gold autumnal leaves
In nature's wrath of gale and storm.

Morgan Woolsey

SPRING HAS SPRUNG
(On seeing the first golden crocus)

Through this first crocus-dawn
   The spring has sprung!
Suddenly, surprisingly, the song is sung
   as treasure gilds the lawn.

Even though winds so chill
   around us blow,
The sun is brave and we reflect its glow
   and hold the promise still.

That promise of our Lord
   that seasons run
Eternal, without change, till life is done,
   according to His Word.

As this first splash of gold
   gladdens the heart,
Our eyes feast hungrily on Nature's art
   and watch new life unfold.

In this bright crocus-day
   the spring is born:
New joy and hope will shine through every dawn
   and will not fade away.

Felicity Plumbley

HIGH SUMMER

Hedgerows are jewelled with roses wild
Among the corn red poppies blow,
Butterflies speed o'er new mown hay,
And forget-me-nots haze the banks below.

Sweet tasselled limes hang down the lane,
And glow-worms light their hedgerow lamps,
Starlings and lapwings begin to flock,
And swallows seek the reed-bed damps.

If Swithin's Day brings rain and clouds
For forty days that will remain -
Or so the wise old folklore tells,
Before hot sun comes back again.

Fallow fields and wastelands wild
Abound with flowers and bracken green,
And woodland foxgloves hang their bells
Where willows by slow waters lean.

July with heady scents of summer
Brings thunderstorms and cooling showers,
Orchards begin to swell their fruits,
And gardens riot with summer flowers.

All silvered by the full moon's touch
The twilight ghost moths flit around,
The night owl glides on silent wings
And swoops its prey without a sound.

Norah M Field

SEASONS OF HEAVEN

What vast array of beauty
Is painted in the skies! -
What myriad range of colours
Await our heavenward eyes!

Dramatic, darkened, splashes
Announce old winter's call -
Sometimes with skies full-laden
With snow about to fall.

The brightness of the morning
In summer's lovely days
Is painted in the heavens
A brightest, bluest haze.

Skies higher seem in springtime
And coloured, purer, blue -
And show us, in creation,
Promise of life anew.

The softened shades of autumn
Touch, almost like caress -
Gold, silent painted heavens
Each gentle soul to bless.

Ah! - Seasons of the heavens
Bring beauty to our land -
And painted for our pleasure
By Heavenly Father's hand.

Dorinda MacDowell

SEASONS OF CHILDHOOD

When I was a child my world was brand new
And I would play under skies of bright blue
Cowslips, buttercups and a sweet daisy chain
The end of a rainbow to search for in vain

Spring in her mantle so colourful and gay
Garlands and dancing on the first day of May
The soft fleece of a lamb in this season of birth
The planting of seeds in this bountiful Earth

With lazy summer days and warm sultry nights
Meadowsweet flowers for a honey bee's delight
Then a flash of lightning and thunder rolled
And I, from my window, watched the storm unfold

Blackberries on hedgerows and crops on the land
A choice of fare from Mother Nature's fair hand
Harvest festival with fruit and gold, rippling corn
A spider's web spangled with dewdrops at dawn

Sparkling Jack Frost and snow, soft and white
A blazing log fire to warm me at night
Holly and mistletoe, a Christmas tree tall
Impatiently waiting for Santa to call

Christmas carols, the nativity, a child's simple faith
Wide-eyed with innocence and daydreams to chase
The seasons of my childhood, the circle of life
A world full of wonder, a world without strife

Sylvia Partridge

AUTUMN

Changing seasons, autumn is here,
It's the most beautiful time of year,
Late summer sun, early morning dew,
Lovely autumn colours are now on view,
Creatures hibernating for winter's sleep,
Snuggling underground, nice and deep.

Wrapping the kids up nice and warm,
Putting a vest under their school uniform,
Motorists cleaning windscreens before they set off,
The early morning chill making them cough,
Not everyone will agree with me I fear,
But I think it's a most beautiful time of year.

Maureen Arnold

October

Even a breath of air
Loosens the chestnut leaves; to ground they go,
Sun-shot with gold. Why, against reason,
Does grief tug at the heart, as each bright frigate
Sets sail for nowhere?
Is it because
Here, in the autumn of age, I see myself
In the helpless pilfered tree, and fear the fall?

Step closer: every empty twig
Is tipped with next year's sticky buds,
You could not see for leaves.

Joy French

PLANTING BULBS

Swifts chatter on my telephone line,
making dates in Sunny Spain.
Wagtails strut across the grass
and bow,
flirting their tails like fans
in a formal minuet.
Blue tits and chaffinches bustle about,
and the crows, those bully-boys,
push each other from the chimney pot
where the warm air strokes their feathers.

A low sun kindles this morning's dew;
the hips and haws and elderberries glow,
ruby and garnet and blood-red cabochons,
against the paling leaves
and still, clear blue
of smiling sky.

I press each corm into the drowsy earth,
each one a minute miracle, a promise made.

Robin, at full concert pitch,
fretsaws the thick, moist air,
harbinger, at umpteen decibels,
of fireside afternoons
with books.

Sarah Ferguson

SUMMER

The sun begins to rise above the rooftops and the trees.
You can hear the birds all singing and the humming of the bees.
You can smell the sweet aroma of the flowers as they bloom
And the smell of fresh-mown grass begins to fill the room.
You can hear the sound of water as it trickles in the pond.
It's as if the Lord above has begun to wave his wand.
Now summer is upon us, things are bright and clear and warm,
We're living in another world and another life is born.

S Brown

DEATH OF A FANTASY

Is this desire's inevitable autumn,
This sudden sharp presentiment
Of cold? Faint aromatic memories
Of distant passion?
Elusive scenes
Of paradise grown old?

No longer need I crave delusion's sunshine;
No longer barefoot in the
Languid heat. Lost enigmatic qualities
Of summer morning -
Hope's futile fantasies
Rest incomplete.

I bid goodbye with pain to summer's fever,
With honesty in torrents
Down my face. Goodbye, my cruel evocative
Illusion - goodbye forever,
Sweet tempestuous place.

And yet I welcome autumn's mellow harvest,
Deep golden evening quietude
To start. I welcome autumn's equinoctial
Beauty - with never,
Never winter in my heart.

Kay Santillo

THE NIGHT

I looked out from the windows
Into the cool, dark, monotonous night
The city lights, far in the distance
Brightened up the skyline.
It was deadly silent,
Suddenly an owl screams
And dives to its innocent prey,
Then silence resumed.
I didn't dare make a noise
In case I interrupted the night.
As I moved slowly the floorboards creaked
I froze not daring even to breathe.
I waited until it was silent again.
The echoes had stopped
The silence was restored.
As I walked out into the open night
I felt as if I'd been swallowed
By the darkness
I carried on walking only stopping occasionally
To make sure nothing was disturbed.
A fox howled in the distance
A crash ripped the silence like a knife
A scream, and a window slammed.
I ran back to the warmth of the house
I closed the door
The floorboards did not creak that time.
But never again will I disturb the night.

Chrissi

THE TOUCH OF AUTUMN

Like the touch of Midas in days of old
autumn turns the leaves to gold
bronze, copper, yellow merge with the green
the most beautiful sight you've ever seen
summer's balmy days have finally gone
now there's a wind-blown carpet to walk upon
but the frost and snow will melt them all away
before the spring they will decay
dissolved into the soil at last
to feed the roots when winter's past
as the days grow longer buds will burst
springtime showers will quench their thirst
until once again a blanket of green
covers the land all fresh and clean
new growth nourished by rain and sun
until
once again the touch of autumn will come . . .

John L Walker

SUBMISSIONS INVITED
SOMETHING FOR EVERYONE

POETRY NOW 2000 - Any subject,
any style, any time.

WOMENSWORDS 2000 - Strictly women,
have your say the female way!

STRONGWORDS 2000 - Warning!
Age restriction, must be between 16-24,
opinionated and have strong views.
(Not for the faint-hearted)

All poems no longer than 30 lines.
Always welcome! No fee!
Cash Prizes to be won!

Mark your envelope (eg *Poetry Now) 2000*
Send to:
Forward Press Ltd
Remus House, Coltsfoot Drive,
Woodston,
Peterborough, PE2 9JX

OVER £10,000 POETRY PRIZES TO BE WON!

Judging will take place in October 2000